Marriage
Together in Christ

by
Joseph Rice

*All booklets are published thanks to the
generous support of the members of the
Catholic Truth Society*

CATHOLIC TRUTH SOCIETY
PUBLISHERS TO THE HOLY SEE

CONTENTS

ACKNOWLEDGMENTS

I have used the generic "man," and "he," to refer to both men and women, partly to streamline the text as much as possible, but mainly to recall the sense of the Hebrew word, "Adam," a word which, meaning "man," does not mean "male," but embraces every member of the human race. Every use of "man" or "he" that is not clearly ascribed to a masculine person in the text ought to be taken as referring equally to either a man or a woman.

The following sources, which are not acknowledged in the text, have nevertheless contributed to this work: I have generally consulted L. Ligier, *Il matrimonio: questioni teologiche e pastorali* (Roma: Città Nuova, 1988), and M. Duggan, *The Consuming Fire: A Christian Introduction to the Old Testament* (San Francisco: Ignatius Press, 1991) in formulating my own argument for relevant portions of the text. I have also benefited greatly from the comments of Fr Francis Martin, and Dr William May, in preliminary drafts. I would also like to acknowledge Fr Miguel Paz, LC, whose systematic approach to teaching the sacrament of Matrimony has influenced the structure of this work.

INTRODUCTION

This is a general introduction to the Catholic perspective on Christian marriage.

Those who are preparing for marriage may find in it an introduction to the deepest meaning of marriage that may help them to prepare to administer the Sacrament more fruitfully to each other so that the life they begin together may be filled with greater joy.

Those who are already married may find in it an opportunity to appreciate more what it means to be married, and how closely they are meant to be joined to each other.

Priests, and all who assist married couples in any way to live this Sacrament may find in it a practical guide to the Church's teaching on the subject.

Those who are not from a Catholic background may find in it an explanation of a Biblical understanding of marriage that may serve as an occasion for a deeper understanding of the mystery through which a man and woman become "one flesh."

These are the hopes with which this book is written. May it be, for all who read it, an occasion to appreciate more this mystery through which a man and a woman become "one flesh."

1. Marriage in the Original Covenant

The Original Gift: Creation

In the beginning, we read in the first chapter of Genesis, God *created* all that exists. To create, in the sense that God alone can create, is to *love something into existence.* It is a tremendously committing step, the joyful, deliberate overflowing of God's goodness. God *knows* all things, even that vast, hidden multitude of things and persons that it would have been possible for Him to create, but that he has decided never to create; God *loves* only those things - and persons - that he has actually chosen to create. It is his love, with all of its original, creative force, that stands as the ground and source of all of our being.

The Original Community:
Man and Woman as God's Image

Male and Female He Created Them

From the beginning, man and woman were created as one, in a call to community that reflects the community of the Trinity: "God created man in his image; in the divine image he created him; male and female he created them" (*Gen* 1:27). God called the first man and woman to be "one flesh," for "it is not good for man to be alone"

(*Gen* 2:18). In heeding this call to community, primarily in marriage and the formation of a family, human beings fully realise their natural vocation to be the image and likeness of God in creation. Thus marriage is the original human community, and even as a natural institution, marriage is meant to be a means of grace both for man and for woman.

> *To create is to love something into existence*

The natural union between the first man and woman was open and free of shame (cf. *Gen* 2:25). Shame is a natural defence, a protective emotion, against the possibility of being used by another person, or reduced to some value, in the eyes of another, that is only a part of our true worth; the presence of shame indicates our perception that this possibility is real (*LR* 174-93; *TB* 114-17). Adam and Eve felt no shame, because there was no risk that they would treat each other with anything less than a full recognition of the true dignity that they shared as the image and likeness of God.

God said, "It is not good for the man to be alone. I will make a suitable helpmate for him" (*Gen* 2:18). Thus we know that the woman was to be the representative of God to the man, for it is God from whom all help comes

God created man in his image; in the divíne image he created him; male and female he created them (Gen 1:27).

to men (*Ps* 121,1-2; cf. *CCC* 1605). Likewise, the man was to represent God to the woman, as her own "helpmate." It was essential, for them to be fully human, that they form a community, within which they would each encounter the Lord.[1]

Building a House for Man

God formed the woman, we read in the second creation account of the Book of Genesis, by "building" her from a rib taken from Adam's side. The Old Testament expression, 'to build a house' for someone, means to provide that person with descendants (cf. *Gen* 16:2; *Ps* 127:1, 3; *Dt* 25:9; *2 Sam* 7:11, 27). It is always, ultimately, God Himself who builds this kind of a house for man.

Animals, when they reproduce, do not need God's creative assistance; there is enough material causality in a male and a female animal to account entirely for the new animal that comes to be. Human beings, however, are spiritual as well as material, and yet a man and a woman contribute only what is material toward the birth of a new child; they contribute the material *conditions* necessary for human life to begin.

It is not true, however, that the man and woman contribute the "body," while God contributes the "soul."

---

[1] Cf. F. Martin, "Marriage in the Old Testament and Intertestamental Periods," in G. W. Olsen (ed.), *Christian Marriage: A Historical Study* (New York: Crossroad, 2001), pp. 1-49, p. 25.

Actually, it is the soul, created by God, that gives both existence and life to the body.[2] The human body is not a pre-existent *container* into which a soul is poured by God; it would be far better to say, in fact, that the body is the material *expression* of the soul. The human parents do, however, still contribute something of the *individuality* of the child, for the new child created by God is really *their* child, too, with specific traits inherited from them. Animals *re-produce;* people *pro-create* - that is, people *assist at an act of creation.*

Profound, Personal Union

The ancient Hebrews had not yet developed an idea of the body as distinct from the soul (in fact, they had no word for "body" as such), and so "flesh" is here meant to describe a union not only of bodies, but of *persons.* "Flesh" is the bond between members of a family, just as we, today, might call family members our own "flesh and blood." This bond of "flesh," in marriage, is even stronger than the same bond that unites a man to his own parents (for "a man leaves his father and mother and clings to his wife, and the two of them become one flesh" (*Gen* 2:24).) It is strong enough, in fact, to be the source of the new bonds of flesh and family that will unite one's descendants for generations.

---

[2] Cf. St Thomas Aquinas, *Quaestiones Disputatae De Malo,* q. 4, a. 4, obj. 6, and response.

When the man calls the woman, "flesh of my flesh," and "bone of my bones," this union is thus linked inseparably to the common bond that unites all human persons, a bond of benevolent love. The man had already named all of the other creatures, as a sign of his dominion and mastery over them; when he saw the woman, however, he first recognised her equality, as "flesh of his flesh," and so he gave her, instead, a special name, one that referred explicitly to the profound, loving relationship of intimacy and equality that the two of them immediately began to share. For Adam and Eve, it was truly, "love at first sight," and Adam, who was "a *man*," called her "*woman*," to express this love.

The name "Adam," means "man," generically, as in "human being." The words "man" and "woman" that Adam used here, however, were specifically masculine and feminine, and he used them to specify the way in which he and his wife were one flesh. In rejoicing that she was "flesh of my flesh," Adam expressed his joy that he had found an equal, feminine spouse, a sign of God's loving presence in his life.

This original unity, experienced first by Adam and Eve, is reproduced in every marriage; as for Adam and Eve, who were naked and felt no shame, there is no need for shame -

for a man leaves his father and mother and clings to his wife, and the two of them become one flesh (Gen 2:24).

i.e., self-defence - in the sexual union of any married couple for whom sex is really an expression of true love.

The Original Blessing: A Two-Fold Mission

God blessed the union of Adam and Eve with the original *nuptial* blessing (*Gen* 1:26-31). He commanded them to be fruitful, to multiply, and to "fill the earth and subdue it" (*Gen* 1:28). They and their descendants were to exercise dominion in his name over all of creation, extending his covenant and his presence to all creatures. Their dual mission to procreate and to govern the world was a mission to continue the work of the Creator, whose Love is the Source and the Purpose of all that exists.

Although this dual mission was revealed to the first man and woman by God, it could also have been discerned, although less clearly, through a reflection on human nature itself. That is why, even in pagan cultures, many ancient matrimonial rites did seek to capture something of the sense of this dual mission. They also perceived that the unity of each married couple was the foundation of the unity of society; marriage became a way for them to forge alliances among families, peoples, and clans.

The original nuptial blessing, with its commands to "be fruitful and multiply," and to "exercise dominion" over all of the earth, was a gift, as well as a mission to be fulfilled. Every human community is founded on the sense that it has its own unique mission, which is always connected in some way to the good that the community is seeking, its common good. Marriage is the original community, and the first, dual mission (to procreate, and to exercise responsible dominion over creation), contained in the original nuptial blessing, was God's wedding gift to the first married couple. *Each* facet of this dual mission implies *both* the unity and the fertility of the couple as two inseparable dimensions of the married vocation, founded in the nuptial blessing.

Marriage is the original community

Throughout the Old Testament, these two dimensions of union and fertility (the unitive and procreative dimensions) were also seen to have their own sacred character. To the Old Testament people of God these dimensions both represented and participated in the spousal covenant-relationship that existed between God and Israel. Just as this covenant gave life to the people of God, so the marriage covenant would also give life to the new members of that people. The blessing of God on the marriage of Adam and Eve enabled them and their descendants to remain faithful to Him and to each other, and to carry out their mission on earth.

The Original Sin

Adam and Eve were placed over all creation, including the animals, because only they could respond freely to the gift that was creation. All the rest of creation is unaware of itself, and determined in its actions. Animals, even when they have a highly developed psychology, are completely material; they are a *part* of the world, acting only by instinct, even when that instinct might be so highly developed - as in a dolphin, for example - as to seem actually "intelligent."

Man is a unity of body *and spirit,* with the *spiritual* capacity to know what is right and to choose it freely. While we experience nature's drives, we are free, when we act, to channel them, or even to act against them. It is this conscious freedom that allowed Adam and Eve to receive creation as an original gift from God, and to offer it back to Him, governing it in a way that reflected the natural state of intimacy that they enjoyed with their Creator; they "walked with God."

We don't exactly know what the material circumstances of Adam and Eve's sin were, but we know that it was a sin of pride, a deliberate failure to live and to walk in the truth. For some mysterious reason, Adam and Eve chose to ignore God's plan, and to impose their own order on creation. Eve, we are told, "saw that the tree was good for food, pleasing to the eyes, and desirable for gaining wisdom" (*Gen* 3:6). What she and her husband chose not to see, however, was the will of God, which was the standard by which both of them were meant to govern the world, and from which all of their authority over creation was derived. Adam and Eve violated the relationship of love, trust, and obedience that bound them so intimately to each other and to God.[3]

This original sin of Adam and Eve, like the loss of a title, or the debt of a squandered fortune, would be inherited, with all of its effects, by all of their descendants.

Consequences of the Original Sin

The greatest consequence of this sin was a hardening of hearts, and a resistance to love. Before the fall, the Source of the love that Adam and Eve shared was the Love of God Himself. When they turned their back on the Source of all love, their own love for each other was also damaged. They could no longer approach each other with such intimacy as before.

Their attitudes toward each other had changed. They no longer found it easy to see each other as a "helpmate," representing God, but now they each experienced an inordinate desire to dominate not only things, but also *persons,* including *each other.* Once, they had experienced their mutual attraction as a source of equality and mutual belonging; now, it was always marred by the possibility that one of them would try to gain the upper hand over the other, especially the man over the woman (*Gen* 3:16). So for the first time, they began to feel *shame,* as a sign of awareness, and a shield, against mutual abuse.

---

[3] I am indebted to Fr Francis Martin for this formulation.

Adam and Eve's sudden loss of intimacy with God also greatly impeded their power of dominion over the earth. They began to suffer pain and hunger. The created world, for the first time in their experience of it, began to resist them, just as they had resisted God, and, for the first time, they had to *work* and *sweat* to earn a living.

Work was actually a blessing in disguise. It required them to struggle within creation instead of naturally lording over it, and so they could once again learn their place, as *creatures,* with respect to God. Work was an antidote for their sin of pride. Pain, fatigue, suffering and death all stand ready to convince us, if we are willing to listen to them, of our need for God. All of the natural evils of this world, if we know how to read them, proclaim the path to the re-establishment of our intimate relationship with God, a path that leads to and through the Cross of Christ.

> *This original sin of Adam and Eve, like the loss of a title, or the debt of a squandered fortune, would be inherited, with all of its effects, by all of their descendants*

The pleasure of sexuality was also damaged by the fall. Not only was the sensual life of Adam and Eve now less intense, but the strong inclination to sin (of all kinds) that they now felt made it harder for them to place their strong desire for each other's *bodies* within the context of their mutual dignity as *persons*. At the same time, sexual pleasure actually *lost* much of the intensity it had for them before they sinned.

One of their descendants would overcome the lying serpent

Childbearing would henceforth be done in pain, and in the context of new difficulties in the relationship between man and wife. Their relationship would now be unequal, and marked by differing desires and expectations (*Gen* 3:16). Their mutual understanding, like the "building of their house" (their descendants), would only be accomplished through a path that included pain and suffering, and their eventual separation through death. God did not design this future for the man and the woman; they chose it for themselves, and for us, by choosing to live apart from Him, the Source of all Love.

The Original Promise: Redemption from Sin

The sins of men are finite; the love of God, infinite. So, while Adam and Eve avoided God after the original sin, God continued to walk in the Garden, in search of them (*Gen* 3:8). God loved them not less, but even more, and he immediately promised them a way of reconciliation with Him.

Adam and Eve would fulfill their dual mission of procreation and governance on earth in the way of suffering that they had chosen; God would continue to "build them a house," and one of their descendants would overcome the lying serpent who had led them away from the Truth. That Descendant - in his created human nature - would be Jesus, Truth Himself.

The Old Testament is the story of God's fidelity to this promise, to his plan of Love and to his original blessing. Within this plan, over the course of salvation history, God's chosen People gradually grew to appreciate the dignity of natural marriage. The woman rejoiced, when she gave birth (*Gen* 4:1), that God was beginning to fulfill his promise. Her child, like every child, represented our eventual triumph, with God, over death. After this first child's birth, Adam began to call her "Eve," "mother of all the living."

God made a covenant with his people in the desert, after bringing them out of slavery in Egypt. This slavery was above all *spiritual,* for they had long forgotten the God of their fathers. In the desert, God restored the relationship he once had with Adam, who "walked" with God, by sharing with them his intimate name, YaHWeH, "I Am Who Am." God, the Ground and Source of our very existence, is also the One who is always with us, who still wishes "to walk" with us, even after we have failed "to walk" with Him.

The Law

In the desert, God gave Israel a Law, to help his chosen people to recognise their need for Him. Under this Law, Israel began to appreciate the unity and the indissolubility of marriage. The Law *gradually* educated Israel away from certain residual effects of the "hardness of hearts" that followed the fall (*CCC* 1610), and toward a fuller understanding of the dignity and complementarity of the spouses. Although the Law tolerated a form of polygamy, and permitted the putting away of one's spouse for certain reasons, adultery was prohibited (cf. *Ex* 20:17; *Lev* 20:10), as were incest and other sexual aberrations (cf. *Lev* 18:6-30; 20:8-21). The People of God was called to "Be holy, for I, Yahweh your God, am holy" (*Lev* 19:2); Jesus would later interpret this call to perfection in light of the universal commandment not only to love, but to love even one's enemies (cf. *Matt* 5:43-48). In the Law, human sexuality was beginning to be re-understood in light of a call to universal love.

In the Ten Commandments, the mutual belonging of one spouse to another is further recognised through the prohibition of the coveting of one's spouse, a prohibition that recognises the sanctity of the relationship between the two.

 Be holy, for I, Yahweh your God, am holy (Lev 19:2).

The final two commandments, which prohibit coveting one's neighbour's wife or one's neighbour's goods, are sometimes superficially juxtaposed, out of context, in order to make the claim that women were somehow considered as "property" in the Old Testament (cf. *Ex* 20:17; *Dt* 5:21). There is no real evidence or basis, however, to support such an interpretation. The purpose of these commandments is not to reinforce the "property" rights of a man, but to prohibit anyone from having an attitude of conniving desire toward that which does not pertain to oneself. If anything, these commandments reinforce the sanctity of the relationship that is already characterised by Adam's exclamation that this one is "flesh of my flesh."[4]

As a further sign of the sanctity the People of God, Hebrew men were prohibited from marrying foreign wives, who might well have been expected to introduce them to the worship of other gods (cf. *Dt* 7:3-4). An exception was made, however, when the woman in question first sincerely converted to the faith of Israel (cf. *Ruth* 1:16).

Marriage and sexuality were interpreted largely in light of the call to purity of the entire People of God and

---

[4] Cf. F. Martin, "Marriage in the Old Testament and Intertestamental Periods," 14-15; cf. et W. Moran, "The Conclusion of the Decalogue," *Catholic Biblical Quarterly* 29 (1967): 543-554.

their commitment to Yahweh. Israel was ever conscious of the importance of the original blessing, and of God's promise of redemption through their descendants, as well as the practical need to have a line of descendants if Israel was to possess the promised land. A man was therefore required to marry his brother's widow, if necessary, to provide him with descendants, if he had failed to father any (*Dt* 25:5-10).

In the Mosaic Law, the Covenant of God with his People and the covenant of marriage *are one and the same*. Both result in the same blessing (cf. *Dt* 7:11-14; 30:19-20), which makes one able to have descendants and to enjoy the fruits of his labours, and which renews the original blessing (*Gen* 1:28). One who keeps the Covenant faithfully and well is richly rewarded with a good and happy marriage and with children (*Ps* 127, 128).

While marriage was threatened and disturbed by the original sin, it was still basically good, and if couples lived it faithfully, giving generously of themselves to each another, it would help them to overcome some of the other effects of the fall, like selfishness and a tendency to live in isolation from community. Having lost its original splendour, the natural marriage of a man and a woman would yet become a prophetic sign as well as an ethical imperative, a task to be realised as part of a renewed fidelity to God's plan.

The Prophets

While the Law seems to emphasise the "procreative" dimension of the Covenant (the line of descendants), the prophets emphasise its "unitive" dimension. For them, the Covenant is a nuptial relationship, in which God is the faithful husband, and Israel is the wife, called to be faithful in return. (cf. *Jer* 3:6-13, 16:9, 25:10, and 31 ff., *Ez* 16, *Hos* 2:21, and *Is* 49:15, ch. 54, and ch. 61-62.)

Prophets speak the mind of God to the present as well as the future, with actions as well as words. Hosea, inspired by God, took an unfaithful wife (a woman who had once participated in a fertility cult to a false god) and gave his three children names that symbolised for Israel the cost of infidelity to God. Hosea's children were illegitimate, not legally, but *religiously,* because they were dedicated to a strange *divinity.* Israel was flirting with the worship of false gods, and Hosea's action was a call to the entire nation to return to the Covenant with God.

The first child was named after the royal court where the fertility cult was practised; God had withdrawn his favour from the royal house. The second was given a name that reflected the whole nation's progressive loss of intimacy with God. When Israel refused to repent, the third child was named "not my people," for God was now *not "I-am"* (that is, *not Yahweh!*) from Israel's point of view. Israel had rejected God and his protection. God, however, would seduce Israel back to Himself (*Hos*

2:16), leading her back to the desert, the place where He had first wooed her, and educated her in the purest love. There, he would offer her not only a restoration of the old covenant, but a new, more intimate covenant, restoring the situation of man before the fall (*Hos* 2:18-25). This new covenant would be reflected in the Sacrament of Matrimony.

Other prophets spoke of the way in which the covenant (and marriage) would be restored. (cf. *Is* 62:5; *Mal* 2:14-16.) The restored relationship would no longer be one of power and inequality (cf. *Jer* 31:33; *Ez* 11:19, 36:26; and *Zac* 12:10, 13:1). The new marriage relationship and the New Covenant would be founded in the truth of *intimacy*.

The Wisdom Books

The wisdom books of the Old Testament recall the original blessing (*Ps* 127, and 128) as a reward for the one who follows in Yahweh's paths (an image that recalls Adam's walking with God) (*Ps* 128:1). Like Abraham, who left his own country to heed God's call and enter into the Covenant, the bride of Psalm 45 is exhorted to forget her nation and ancestral home, to marry the king, and to receive from him descendants who will rule the world. These books praise marital fidelity (*Prov* 5:19) and counsel against adultery (*Prov* 30:20, *Eccl* 9), and praise the value of a perfect wife, as "far beyond the price of pearls" (*Prov* 31:10).

The *Song of Songs,* a series of love-poems, tells a story of human and divine love in the intimate context of the New Covenant, in which every husband and wife would treat each other as "flesh of my flesh." The mutual recognition of the truth about each other brings harmony and fascination, expressed in the "language of the body" to the marital relationship (*TB* 368-70). The bride exclaims, "I am my Beloved's, and his desire is for me," and thus restores the imbalance (*Gen* 3:16) that followed the fall: a wife, in God's plan, is never a mere possession of the husband, but a person to be loved and respected with a freedom founded in truth (*TB* 370-75). The bridegroom invites her to "set me like a seal upon your heart, like a seal on your arm. For love is strong as Death, jealousy relentless as Sheol" (*Songs* 8:6). His invitation signifies a relationship in which God Himself is present, one as intimate as it is *indissoluble* (cf. *Jer* 22:24; *Esther* 8:7-8; cf. *John* 1:14).

In the book of Tobit, a young couple, Tobias and Sarah, must, in order to be united forever, overcome a threat of death that stems from the devil's destructive hatred for marriage as the image of the Covenant. By facing their trial with faith, hope, and love, this couple learns a love that is even *stronger* than death. Their prayer of thanksgiving recalls the original blessing of God, and his fidelity to his promise; in it, Tobias calls Sarah his "sister bride," an expression that signifies their call to intimacy as "one flesh."

It was you who created Adam
you who created Eve to be his wife
to be his help and support;
and from these two the human race was born.
It was you who said,
 It is not good that the man should be alone;
let us make him a helpmate like himself.
And so I do not take my sister for any lustful motive;
I do it in singleness of heart. (Tobit 8:5-7; cf. TB 375-77).

The Hebrew Liturgy

The liturgical dimension of marriage begins with a
promise and ends in a common life. We find these two
dimensions reflected in the Hebrew liturgy of marriage in
the Old Testament, (cf. *Gen* 24; *Tob* 7-13) which had
two phases. The first, was the betrothal, with a blessing,
a promise, and a sign (usually a ring). The second was
the wedding itself, when the bride entered to become part
of the groom's house. The Hebrew wedding liturgy
commemorated the moment of creation and of the
original blessing, and contained in itself a hope of the
final restoration to come.

2. MARRIAGE IN THE NEW COVENANT

A Supernatural Gift, from God and Man to each Man

The New Testament, or Covenant, fulfilled the Old in the person of Jesus Christ. Through the Incarnation and the Redemption, Jesus *restored* our fallen human nature, and *elevated* it to a new, *super*natural level. He, the promised Descendant of the marriage of Adam and Eve, the Son of Abraham and of David, fulfilled in his own person both the prophetic dimension of the marital covenant, and the original blessing. For this reason, he often used the phrase "Son of Man" (literally, "Son of *Adam*") to refer to Himself as the Messiah, the One who was to come.

Jesus also revealed that he is the Son of *God*. The New Covenant that he came to institute would be based on a new law, a law of Love, and so it would also be an invitation to intimate participation in the life of the Blessed Trinity. A new and powerful dignity would be communicated to each person who entered into the New Covenant, a dignity which would enable each one to communicate God to others, loving them with the Love that is God Himself.

A New and Supernatural Dignity for Marriage

As the image of the covenant, marriage itself was also not only restored, but elevated. The natural institution of marriage, given to man in the Old Covenant, was a means of *actual* grace (i.e., God *helping* us in our spiritual and temporal needs) to assist spouses in their life together, so now the supernatural institution of marriage, that is, the *sacrament of Matrimony,* instituted by Jesus, would become a means of *sanctifying* grace (i.e., God Himself *living* within us), to enable spouses to participate more fully in the divine life of the Trinity, according to the New Covenant.

Baptism is the sacrament by which persons enter into the New Covenant, and Matrimony is the sacrament that mirrors and perpetuates it. In its unitive dimension, the sacrament of Matrimony represents and makes us participants in the New Covenant, the marriage of Jesus, the Bridegroom, with his Bride, the Church (cf. *Matt* 9:15, 22:2, 25:1ff; *John* 3:29; *CCC* 1612); in its procreative dimension, the sacrament of Matrimony gives life to new generations, who are a line of descendants of the People of God.

On the threshold of his public life Jesus performs his first sign - at his mother s request - during a wedding feast. The Church attaches great importance to Jesus presence at the wedding at Cana. She sees in it the confirmation of the goodness of marriage and the proclamation that thenceforth marriage will be an efficacious sign of Christ s presence (CCC 1612).

Jesus, the Bridegroom, begins his public life by changing water into wine at the wedding at Cana, thereby confirming the goodness of marriage, and proclaiming that marriage will thereafter be an efficacious sign of his presence (cf. *John* 2:1-11; *CCC* 1613). Recalling the way it was "from the beginning," Jesus rejects the practice of divorce, a lingering sign of the "hardness of hearts" that resulted from the fall, and proclaims instead that "what God has united, man must not divide" (*Matt* 19:1-9). As the Bridegroom, and the promised Descendant, he has come to restore all things to the way God made them "in the beginning."

Just as natural marriage began as a participation in God's original plan for creation, Jesus elevated marriage to the level of a sacrament, making it a form of participation in the Kingdom of Heaven. St Paul, referring to the new life of baptised persons, who have been incorporated into the Body of Christ, used to use the phrase, to live "in the Lord" (*1 Cor* 7:39; *Rom* 16:2, 8:11-12; *Eph* 4:17; *Eph* 6:10; *1 Thess* 5:12; *et al.*). Nothing could describe the union of two Christian spouses better than to say that they are married "in the Lord."

Marriage as a Sign of Our Longing for the Kingdom

Every marriage between a man and a woman exists only in this life, for the same reason that faith and hope exist only in this life: marriage is a way of preparation and anticipation toward what is to come. Faith and hope pass away once they are fulfilled in the vision of God, for there is no longer any need for them; every Christian marriage passes away once it is fulfilled in the final realisation, in the experience of one of the spouses, of the marriage between Christ, the Bridegroom, and his Church, which, in the end, is experienced uniquely by each member of the Church.

The fact that Christian marriage does not outlast the death of one of the spouses should not be a motive for disappointment for the many happily married couples, each of which naturally desires that its union last forever. We have already witnessed, in Tobit, a love that is *stronger* than death, and so we should also expect the love of Christian marriage, in some way, to outlast death. It is not that one ceases, at death, to experience the love that was present in marriage; rather, one goes on to experience it fully, and perfectly, in Christ, and so perfectly that it would be impossible to be any closer - or, even, *to feel* any closer, to one's earthly spouse than one is able to be - and to experience - through being completely united to Christ.

Just as marriage is a participation in the New Covenant, so perseverance in fidelity to one spouse is a participation in that fidelity that led Jesus to persevere to the end on the Cross. "It is by following Christ, renouncing themselves, and taking up their crosses that spouses will be able to 'receive' the original meaning of marriage and live it with the help of Christ. This grace of Christian marriage is a fruit of Christ's cross, the source of all Christian life" (*CCC* 1615; *Matt* 19:11).

Baptism makes a human person a sanctuary of the Holy Spirit. Sexual intercourse outside of marriage is a sin against one's own body, as well as a sin against the Body of Christ (*1 Cor* 6:12-20). It is also a denial of one's own true dignity as an *incarnate spirit,* for whom the act of sexual intercourse should have great and permanent meaning as an act of love.

The Holy Spirit is Love itself; no act of sexuality that grieves the Holy Spirit can ever be an act of true love. Fidelity to one's spouse *before* marriage is an eloquent expression of the fidelity to Christ that marks the New Covenant, and the expectation of the entire Church for that covenant to be fulfilled. St Paul expresses this expectation when he tells the members of the Church at Corinth, "I arranged for you to marry Christ so that I might give you away as a chaste virgin to this one husband" (*2 Cor* 11:2).

Marriage as a Mystery of Identification with Christ

The meaning of the marriage of a man and a woman, in God's plan, is intimately connected with God's own covenant with man:

Give way to one another in obedience to Christ. Wives should regard their husbands as they regard the Lord, since as Christ is head of the Church and saves the whole body, so is a husband the head of his wife; and as the Church submits to Christ, so should wives to their husbands, in everything. Husbands should love their wives just as Christ loved the Church and sacrificed himself for her to make her holy. He made her clean by washing her in water with a form of words, so that when he took her to himself she would be glorious, with no speck or wrinkle or anything like that, but holy and faultless. In the same way, husbands must love their wives as they love their own bodies; for a man to love his wife is for him to love himself. A man never hates his own body, but he feeds it and looks after it; and that is the way Christ treats the Church, because it is his body - and we are its living parts. *For this reason, a man must leave his father and mother and be joined to his wife, and the two will become one body.* [Gen 2:24] This mystery has many implications; but I am saying it applies to Christ and the Church. To sum up; you too, each one of you, must love his wife as he loves himself; and let every wife respect her husband (Eph 5:21-33).

It would be a great mistake, as well as a lack of appreciation for Sacred Scripture as the Word of God, to see this passage as some sort of an outdated reflection of the cultural conditions under which St Paul was writing, reflecting a society based on male domination. It would also be quite the opposite of what St Paul - and the Holy Spirit - is intending. By clearly referring to the way it was *in the beginning* and quoting the Book of Genesis, St Paul is specifically rejecting a relationship between husband and wife that is based on domination and lust.

The key to the whole passage is found in the first sentence, "Give way to one another in *obedience* to Christ." Obedience, which may be the most misunderstood virtue of our time, has nothing to do with a caricature of submission and domination, and everything to do with the mutual surrender of intimacy through *faith* in Jesus Christ, whom each of the spouses represents to the other. In fact, the original word used means also "reverence." Christian obedience is always and only "the obedience of faith" (cf. *CCC* 144-49). "To obey (from the Latin *ob-audire,* to 'hear or listen to') in faith is to submit freely to the word that has been heard, because its truth is guaranteed by God, who is Truth itself" (*CCC* 144). Obedience is based on the intimacy of one's relationship with God; it implies not so much *blind submission,* as *generous comprehension,* based on *faith.* For the same reason, one is never obliged (or excused) by obedience to commit sin; obedience against God is not true obedience.

Marriage as a Mystery of Fruitful Love

Once Christ has restored and elevated marriage, the love that *mysteriously* animates every Christian marriage is now the Love of God Himself, the Holy Spirit, in Person. It is not only the *image* of the love with which Christ sacrifices Himself for the Church and the Church adheres unfailingly to the will of Christ, *but it is the exact same love.* This is the *mystery* of faith to which St Paul refers: he exhorts Christian spouses not only to *imitate* the love between Christ and the Church, *but to live it.*

That is why the passage from Ephesians may even be the most relevant passage in all of Scripture for Christian married couples today. It requires both husband and wife to endeavour to appreciate each other more and more fully, and to surrender to each other completely, within an accurate understanding of the fundamental difference contained in being "male and female." It is not about *roles,* but about *sexuality,* which is not a social construct, but an intimate part of who each of us is. Our sexuality permeates everything we do; each of us is always acting either as a man or as a woman, even though some acts clearly involve our sexuality more than others. Pope John Paul II has commented, for example, that:

> Sexuality, by means of which man and woman give themselves to one another through the acts which are proper and exclusive to spouses, is by no means

something purely biological, but concerns the innermost being of the human person as such. It is realised in a truly human way only if it is an integral part of the love by which a man and a woman commit themselves totally to one another until death (FC 11).

The passage from Ephesians is not an endorsement of the relegation of women to second-class status. In fact, it is up to each couple to determine what specific form the living out of the beautiful complementarity of being "male and female," will take. In some areas, there is more latitude than others in setting the roles that a man and a woman will play within the married relationship. Only the man can be a father, and only the woman can be a mother; the needs of their children, at different ages, must therefore be carefully considered. On the other hand, there are other, less transcendent, areas in which the individual talents and temperaments of the spouses may be much more important than their sexuality.

St Paul refers, in the same passage, to the "mystery" of Christian marriage within the context of the mystical union between Christ and the Church, which is his Body (*Eph* 5:31-32). Christian marriage, the image of the New Covenant, also reflects and participates in the mystery of our Redemption, the mystery that sealed the New Covenant, in both its unitive and procreative dimensions.

In its unitive dimension, Christian marriage reflects the totality of Christ's loving gift of Himself to his Church; Christian marriage is a union of persons, not just of their bodies, but of their entire earthly lives. In its procreative dimension, marriage reflects the spiritual "fertility" of the People of God. The primary fertility of a Christian marriage is not limited to childbearing alone, but extends also to a participation in the spiritual fertility of the Church, bringing new members into the Body of Christ.

> *Those who enter into marriage "in the Lord," form, with their children, a "domestic Church."*

Through the Church, Jesus, the new Adam, accomplishes the mission to exercise responsible dominion over all the earth (cf. *Eph* 1:22-23); with the Church, he also exercises the mission to procreate, generating new life, in the Holy Spirit, through the rebirth of human persons "from above" (cf. *John* 3:4-8). The Church is the "house" that God builds upon the earth, the house of the Lord, his Temple and his line of descendants (cf. *Eph* 2:19-22; 4:15-16). Thus the original blessing, "Be fruitful, multiply, fill the earth and conquer it" (*Gen* 1:28), is fulfilled *both* in the Church as a whole, and in every Christian marriage.[5]

---

[5] A similar spiritual fertility, in the heart of the Church, must be ascribed to virginity or celibacy "in the Lord." Marriage, and virginity or celibacy, are the two ways of participating in the *building-up* of the Kingdom of God on earth.

The baptised man and woman, thus already mystically espoused with Christ in the Church, who enter into marriage "in the Lord," form, with their children, a "domestic Church." Each "domestic Church" is the "living image," the "historical representation," and the "specific revelation and realisation" of the ecclesial communion of the Church as a whole. Each "domestic Church," like the Church as a whole, must, therefore, continually grow in an understanding of the plan of God over itself; parents and spouses have a particular duty and responsibility not only to educate their children, but to evangelise their own families and each other *constantly, intensely,* and *permanently* (*FC* 21, 49, and 51). As the "dignity and responsibility that belongs to the Christian family as the domestic Church can be achieved only with God's unceasing aid," the family *must* learn to pray together if it is to fulfill its mission, and the primary educational responsibility of parents toward their children will always be that of teaching them to pray (*FC* 59-60).

3. MARRIAGE AS A SACRAMENT
IN THE HEART OF THE CHURCH

Gradual Understanding Of Sacramentality

The Church has gradually advanced in its understanding of what it means for Matrimony to be a sacrament. The Holy Spirit works in His Body, the Church (CCC 1116), through the sacraments, which are efficacious signs of God's grace, instituted and entrusted to the Church by Jesus Himself (*CCC* 1131; cf. 1113 ff). *"In the beginning,"* before the fall, all created things once exercised a "primordial sacramentality"; man, through their use, naturally grew in friendship with God. Now that all things have been restored by Christ through His Incarnation, the seven sacraments have become both the source and the apex of the *recovered sacramentality* of all created things: *all* created things can lead to, signify, or communicate Christ, *through* the seven sacraments as means of grace (*CCC* 1084). Every marriage can lead us to Christ, through the power of the Sacrament of Matrimony.

The effectiveness of the sacraments is based on the power of God Himself, derived from the Incarnation of the Word, and mediated through the human nature of Jesus Christ and through the minister of each sacrament.[6] They do not depend on the faith of the individual who receives them; anyone who receives a sacrament without faith or without being in the state of grace will not receive the fullness of sacramental grace right away, but will receive it once that obstacle ceases to exist, for the *power* of the sacrament has already been received.[7] On the other hand, the sacraments are in no way *magical;* magic involves the use of human rituals to *control* nature or to manipulate its forces, whereas the sacraments involve a free gift of God's grace to man.

The Church recognises seven sacraments (*CCC* 1210). All of them were instituted by Christ Himself, and are grounded in Sacred Scripture; all of them are ordered to the Eucharist, the "Sacrament of sacraments," as to their end (*CCC* 1211).[8] The Church's theological reflection on these sacraments, like all of its theological reflection, has matured over time, even to this present day. For example, the very term, "sacrament," was often used in a wider sense, in earlier times, to include many rituals of the Church, but its usage was gradually clarified and limited to the seven sacraments over the centuries.

Among the seven sacraments, there are two, Holy Orders and Matrimony, that are "sacraments of communion," that is, they are directed toward the

---

[6] Cf. Aquinas, *Summa Theologiae* III, q. 48, a. 6; cf. et q. 60 ff.
[7] Cf. *ibid.,* III, q. 63.
[8] Cf. *ibid.,* III, q. 65, a. 3.

salvation of others, and not only ourselves. While all members of the Church are *consecrated,* through Baptism and Confirmation, for "the common priesthood of the faithful," it is through Holy Orders and Matrimony that they may also receive *particular consecrations* reflecting their particular mission in the Church and the way that they are each called to build up the Body of Christ (*CCC* 1534-35). Through Matrimony, "Christian spouses are fortified and, as it were, *consecrated* for the duties and dignity of their state" (*GS* 48).

Gradual Understanding of Marriage as Sacrament

The Church essentially realised from the very beginning that marriage was what it would later call a "sacrament." As with other sacraments, however, the full consciousness, in every detail, of what it meant for marriage to be a sacrament, as well as a separate liturgical rite for it, underwent its own gradual

In the Latin Church, it is ordinarily understood that the spouses, as ministers of Christ s grace, mutually confer upon each other the sacrament of Matrimony by expressing their consent before the Church. In the eastern liturgies the minister of this sacrament (which is called Crowning) is the priest or bishop who, after receiving the mutual consent of the spouses, successively crowns the bridegroom and the bride as a sign of the marriage covenant (CCC 1623).

development. Certain elements found also in non-Christian marriage rituals were adapted and assimilated, and Christian prayers and symbolism were added to them. Eventually, by at least the Fifth Century, a separate liturgical rite for a wedding Mass had begun to exist. Today, that rite has undergone a parallel development in the East and the West; certain legitimate differences exist between the two traditions regarding the importance of the blessing and the identity of the minister of the sacrament (*CCC* 1623).

Some of the questions that were raised and answered by the Church had to do with identifying what the essential requirements for marriage were; for example, whether it was necessary to have a dowry (and, if so, who should have to pay it), or to have the permission of the bride's parents; or whether the priest's blessing was a necessary part of the sacrament itself. There were also other questions that had to do with identifying essential elements of the Sacrament, such as the vows, the exchange of consent, and the consummation.

The Church was always at least implicitly conscious, however, that Christian marriage is a sacrament. This consciousness gradually became more and more explicit through the evolution of Church law, the Church's responses to doctrinal questions, the development of sacramental theology, and various statements of the Magisterium; as the Church understood more and more *what* it was to be a sacrament, it also, naturally, understood more and more *how* marriage is a sacrament.

From around the Tenth Century, the Church began progressively to assert its right to legislate about marriage independently of the state. The first *explicit and thematic* mention of marriage as a sacrament, however, took place in 1124 at the Synod of Chartres.

The Place of Marriage and the Family in the Heart of the Church

In the life of the Church, married couples exercise a specific ministry that incorporates the two missions given to Adam and Eve in the *original nuptial blessing,* the missions to *pro*-create, and to exercise dominion over the earth. Married couples are "called to illuminate and organise temporal realities according to the plan of God, Creator and Redeemer" (*FC* 5). Physically, procreation is not always possible; the attitude of *parenthood,* however, that is, of a generous openness to life that is reflected in the willing assumption of responsibility toward others in need, even when radiating a fertility that consists primarily in charity, hospitality, and sacrifice,[9] is always possible and essential to any marriage:

---

[9] Cf. K. Wojtyla, "The Radiation of Fatherhood," in *The Collected Plays and Writings on Theater,* tr. B. Taborski (Berkeley: University of California Press, 1987), pp. 333-68.

> Even when procreation is not possible, conjugal life does
> not for this reason lose its value. Physical sterility in fact can
> be for spouses the occasion for other important services to
> the life of the human person, for example, adoption, various
> forms of educational work, and assistance to other families
> and to poor or handicapped children (*FC* 14).

Moreover, "the fundamental task of marriage and family is to be at the service of life"; parents educate their children, and bear fruit by handing on to them "moral, spiritual, and supernatural life" (*CCC* 1653). As the domestic Church, this triple life radiates throughout society from within the family.

The family is called to return to the "beginning," to the creative Fatherhood of God, and to radiate this Fatherhood throughout society. The primary way for a family to witness to the Love of God is to become more and more what it already is, an intimate community of life and love that reflects the life and love of the Blessed Trinity, present in the world. Thus "the family has the mission to guard, reveal and communicate love, and this is a living reflection of and a real sharing in God's love for humanity and the love of Christ the Lord for the Church His bride." This mission, toward which the family is urged on by Love, embraces four general tasks: "1) forming a community of persons; 2) serving life; 3) participating in the development of society; [and] 4) sharing in the life and mission of the Church" (*FC* 17 ff).

Every family shares in the mission to be an intimate community of life and love; the family of two baptised spouses, whose marriage is a sacrament, a means of sanctifying grace for themselves and for the world, fulfills this mission in a particular way, from the very heart of the Church, and witnesses to the truth about God's plan for the family and for creation.

4. The Ethics of Marriage and Family

First Principles

The mission of the married couple and the family in the Church may be seen, perhaps, more clearly in light of the ethical requirements of the natural law. "Natural law" is a phrase used to describe the most basic moral and ethical principles, so basic that no one in his right mind would call them into question. They are natural because they reflect human nature, that is, the way of being and acting that is essentially human; they are a "law" because they reflect the original plan for the world of the Creator, what is sometimes called the Eternal Law. They are not revealed, like divine Law (for example, the Ten Commandments), but *discerned* through a careful reflection about the way things are. The natural law, like a set of instructions for a new car, helps us to get the most out of our lives, and to avoid major breakdowns along the way.

The most basic principle of the natural law is that all men should "do good, and avoid evil." Closely allied to this principle, there are four other principles that derive from it. All men should (1) seek to preserve life, (2) seek to preserve the human species, (3) seek the truth, and (4) seek to live in community. The mission of every marriage and every family, to be an intimate community of life and love, and its four general tasks, are clearly connected with the natural law. The Christian family, a loving community at the *service of life*, builds up society at the same time it builds up the Body of Christ, fulfilling both missions given by God "in the beginning," the mission to procreate, and the mission to exercise responsible dominion over the earth.

The Christian family, a loving community at the service of life

Ethics is not about limiting human choices, but about discovering principles that will guide us to become what we are. True ethical imperatives, like the natural law itself, are inherently positive, even when they are negatively formulated; they are, first of all, principles of growth and maturity, and only secondarily principles of avoiding evil. There are certain ethical imperatives that follow for the Christian marriage and family both from the natural law and the original blessing.

Respect for Life

From the natural imperatives to preserve life and to preserve the species, it follows that the Christian couple and their family must have an absolute respect for life at all stages, but especially at those stages when a person is most defenceless, that is, in the womb, in a state of mental or physical weakness, or during the often gradual approach of natural death. Obviously, abortion and euthanasia, the direct taking of innocent life, can never be justified in any form. Occasionally, however, parents or children may have to make choices regarding the use of extraordinary medical procedures, such as the removal of a cancerous womb, or the provision of a sufficient dose of pain relief to a suffering patient, even though the hastened death of an unborn child or an aging parent may be the foreseeable, although unintended result. These cases are not truly cases of abortion or euthanasia. When in doubt, however, a competent theologian, known to live in intimate communion with the teaching authority of the Church, should be consulted before taking any steps that may implicate the life of another, even indirectly.

Less obviously, contraception is also an anti-life act, for it seeks to change the meaning of sexual intercourse from a loving, life-giving act to a sterile, self-centred act. It is *contra* the *conception* of a new *life*.[10]

To Live in the Truth

From the natural imperative to seek the truth, it follows that Christian spouses must constantly and energetically

---

[10] Cf. W. May, "Contraception and the Culture of Death," in *Marriage and the Common Good: Proceedings of the 22nd Annual Convention of the Fellowship of Catholic Scholars,* ed. K . Whitehead (South Bend, Indiana: St Augustine's Press, 2001), pp. 173-203.

evangelise each other and the members of their family, as the greatest truth is Jesus, the living Truth, in Person. Having received this Truth as a free gift, it is imperative to seek, as St Paul puts it, to "learn Christ" (*Eph* 4:20); as Christians, we have three duties with regard to our faith: (1) to receive it generously, as a gift that also commits us to action; (2) to assimilate it, radically, and open to all of its consequences; (3) to transmit it, through our words and actions of love, and above all, through the testimony of our lives. Parents are the primary educators of their children in all spheres, but especially when it comes to prayer; parents must not only *teach* their children to pray, but must *pray with each other and with them.* It is *prayer* that teaches us what it means for each of us to be himself, makes us one with the Truth, and teaches us to love the One who is Good, God Himself. It is prayer that is the source of the strength of the family (*LF* 4).

To Live as Family

The natural imperative to live in community is experienced primarily in the family, which is the primordial, or most basic community. One of the Psalms likens the experience of living in community, as one family, to a rite of consecration in which oil is poured on the head of the high priest and God lavishes his blessings on his people (*Ps* 133). The family, the domestic Church, is the primary community, willed by God, as an image of the Trinity, and as a means of grace for the world. Peace in the family, especially in the Christian family, is the root of peace in the world. At times, given the ups and downs of life, and our imperfect condition after the fall, building the family into the kind of loving community that it is meant to be is hard work, and requires sacrifice and persevering commitment.

Every marriage, and every family, will face challenges, because life is challenging. The imperative to live in community requires the members of a family to seek to help each other to meet those challenges, and to avoid creating challenges for the others through selfish acts or attitudes. The most fundamental challenge for every married spouse or member of a family is the daily challenge of learning to empty oneself, as Christ did (*Phil* 2:7), in order to make others happy. Conversely, many problems arise when something, especially something sinful, but at times even something good in itself, becomes more fundamental to a person than his bond to his spouse and his family. The thing in question could be as terrible as a drug addiction, or as seemingly innocuous as playing a game of golf at the wrong time; to the extent that it interferes with the life of one's family, it interferes with one's own reason for being, one's own happiness.

The key to living in peace, within marriage and the family, is to depend on God. Again, this requires prayer and a constant commitment to living in the truth. Anxiety, doubt, and fear are never from God; nor is any desire that ends up by distracting a person from the true living of his vocation to marriage and the family. There is a natural joy that permeates the lives of couples and families who live "in the Lord" (cf. *Phil* 4:4-7); because they are deeply in touch with who they are, and with what a great thing it is to be a child of God, they know how to put everything else in its place, and not to be consumed with worry over the troubles of each day (cf. *Matt* 6:25-34).

Every community is centred on a gift and mission that is held in common, a common good. When a spouse or a member of the family is not faithful to this mission that unites the domestic community, the peace of the entire family can be threatened. Infidelity, in fact, is often *felt* before it is *known*. When infidelity, in what ever form, becomes a serious threat to the marriage or family, or to one of its members, or when it gravely impedes the ability of the family to fulfill its mission, the separation from the daily life of the family of a spouse or, less

I want you to be happy, always happy in the Lord; I repeat, what I want is your happiness. Let your tolerance be evident to everyone: the Lord is very near. There is no need to worry; but if there is anything you need, pray for it, asking God for it with prayer and thanksgiving, and that peace of God, which is so much greater than we can understand, will guard your hearts and your thoughts, in Christ Jesus (Phil 4:4-7).

frequently, of an abusive child, may be warranted for a time. Prudence and charity, together with good, even professional, advice, are essential for knowing how to proceed in such delicate situations.

Human Sexuality

Because human sexuality involves the whole person, and not just certain dimensions of the person, sexuality also involves all four of these natural law principles.

> *Marital fidelity begins before marriage, with a willingness to wait until the marriage is real and permanent*

Truth is a fundamental condition for sexual intimacy to be real, and not an illusion. True love is never temporary, and true sexual intimacy is never found outside of marriage.

Because it is not a true expression of love, sexual intimacy before marriage can threaten the perseverance of a relationship; even if marriage eventually follows, couples who live together before marriage are at least 33% and up to 80% (in some parts of Europe) more likely to divorce than those who do not.[11] Marital fidelity begins *before* marriage, with a willingness to wait until the marriage is real and permanent.

----

[11] Cf. M. A. Wilson, *Love and Family: Raising a Traditional Family in a Secular World* (San Francisco: Ignatius Press, 1996), p. 122.

The union of any man and woman as "one flesh" (*Gen* 2:24) is not only expressed but also brought about through their bodily union in sexual intercourse. This ability to form a bond so intimate that it is capable of uniting one's descendants for generations to come is an integral part of God's loving plan for creation. In fact, however, this bond of flesh and family is necessarily formed in *each* and *every* act of sexual intercourse, for in it, the man and woman enter into a relationship with each other in which they might become *parents,* often, due to biological factors, without ever even knowing it. The "one flesh" that is formed in this way *always* includes *parenthood* as an integral dimension of the sexual act. St Paul, in fact, explicitly affirms that every act of sexual intercourse, even with a prostitute, makes a man and a woman "one flesh" (*1 Cor* 6:16). That is why sexual intercourse outside of marriage is always such a great violation of human dignity, and not only of the dignity of those performing it; it also displays a callous disregard toward the dignity of one's own potential descendants, who have a right to be loved and welcomed into existence within the bonds of a true and intact family.

Likewise, any use of sexuality that does not respect life in its beginnings, including the right of the child to come to be according to the way God inscribed into its own nature, can lead spouses and family members to fall away from each other and from God. Human cloning, in-vitro fertilisation, and other techniques that fail to respect the intimate connection between procreation and sexual relations fall into this category; various other techniques of assisting procreation that may respect this connection are becoming available as technology advances, and some of these may, in time, be judged to be licit. The use of such inhuman techniques to manufacture *children,* however, has already led to a frightening catastrophe, as many embryonic *children* have been abandoned by their often now-divorced parents to life and death sentences under cold, antiseptic laboratory conditions, without ever experiencing the warmth of human love and acceptance to which they, as *persons,* are entitled. They are *persons,* no matter how small and vulnerable they may be.

Marital sexual intercourse, when properly lived, is an act in which a man and his wife come together to assist, potentially, at the creation of a new, individual human life; it is an act, especially within the sacrament of Matrimony, that recalls the creation of the world and its renewal in the Holy Spirit (cf. *Ps* 104:30), and effectively symbolises the union that exists between Christ and his Church. It is meant to be a grace-filled act, one through which the Love of God is poured out into the world.

The source of the love and creative potential in this act is God Himself. To attempt, through the use of contraceptive methods or means, to separate the experience of loving sexual union from the possibility that a new

human person might be created by God, is an aberration
that destroys the *union* of the married couple as well as the
procreative dimension of the act. (Here we are speaking
within the context of marriage; contraceptive intercourse
outside of marriage is an even more complex situation,
involving several evils at once, and potentially with a very
detrimental effect, in the long term, on each person and his
ability to commit himself in love to another.) Contraception
destroys the *union* of the couple because it cuts them off
from the Source of their union in the very act that is
supposed to establish and build up their union; the Source
of their union and of their creative potential is One and the
Same. It is thus always false to oppose the *unitive*
dimension of marriage to the *procreative* dimension in a
kind of balancing act to achieve a rough proportion
between good and evil. What destroys the one also destroys
the other. They are inseparable.

Responsible paternity

Human sexuality is closely linked to the natural
imperative to live in community. One area in which this
imperative comes into play is that of *responsible
paternity*. Just because contraception always tends to
destroy a marriage does not mean that married couples
must always procreate at every opportunity. In fact,
spouses have a duty to their children, to whom they
assume a commitment to raise and educate them, as well

as a duty to each other, to space the arrival of their children according to their means and their human potential in every dimension. As marriage is intrinsically ordered to procreation and fertility, it would be wrong to marry with the intention of never having any children at all; in fact, it would invalidate the marriage. On the other hand, having children too quickly or too often can even be harmful to the health of the mother or the children.

It is fairly easy for spouses to discern the woman's cycle of fertility. Indeed, there are only about one-hundred hours during each month in which it is possible for a woman to conceive. Some methods of *natural family planning*, such as the Billings method, or the sympto-thermal method, can accurately pinpoint that cycle down to a margin of error of one or two days; others, such as the Hilgers method, are so accurate as to pinpoint it within the space of a few hours. (These methods are not to be confused with the old "rhythm" or "calendar" methods, which were less accurate, for they were not so personalised to each woman's cycle.) Natural family planning methods, which can be learned, in practice, over the space of a few weeks, are more than 98% effective at avoiding pregnancy, when used for that purpose. These same methods are also quite effective at *achieving* pregnancy, for example, by helping a couple to plan to have intercourse at the most fertile moment possible; couples who wish to achieve pregnancy are normally able to do so within three cycles.

Above all, natural family planning methods are good for the longevity of a marriage. While the great majority of marriages that end in divorce have involved the use of contraception, the divorce rate among couples practising natural family planning is normally in the low single digits. In fact, while more than 50% of all marriages today end in divorce, only 2% to 5% of couples using natural family planning ever divorce.[12] Natural family planning encourages the husband to become an equal partner in the sexual relationship, understanding the woman's body, her hormonal cycle, and her emotional needs much better than he otherwise would. It also teaches couples to appreciate the value of ways of being physically intimate, as man and wife, without needing to proceed to a sexual climax. Finally, natural family planning, when done well, can greatly enhance communication in a marriage.

Natural family planning encourages the husband to become an equal partner in the sexual relationship

These natural methods are easily as effective as any contraceptive available today. For the same reasons that contraception is always wrong, however, natural methods may not legitimately be used with a contraceptive intent, such as to avoid pregnancy

---

[12] Cf. *ibid.,* p. 261.

absolutely. Nor may one use the natural methods to pinpoint fertile days, and then use a contraceptive to engage in intercourse on those days. Such practices are dishonest and self-contradictory, as well as simply wrong, and cannot help the couple to grow as one.

The principle behind these natural methods is simple; it is that spouses may responsibly choose when - or when not - to exercise their right to engage in marital sexual intercourse as long as they remain *open* to the possibility of pregnancy and willing to accept a baby if God creates one. Contraception is totally inconsistent with this principle. As long as the couple is not intending to avoid pregnancy absolutely throughout their marriage, and as long as their reasons for spacing their children are good and serious ones, however, there is nothing wrong with using the infertile days of the woman's cycle and avoiding the fertile ones. In fact, sometimes it can even be *imperative* to do so, when, for example, due to a woman's precarious state of health, pregnancy might even be dangerous.

Unlike natural methods, every contraceptive method available today actually *diminishes* the pleasure of sexual intercourse in some way. Some are mechanical; others interfere with a woman's hormonal cycle. All of them, moreover, can be expected to increase anxiety, for none are totally safe.[13] Many, in fact, carry an increased risk of

---

[13] Cf. *ibid.*, p. 143.

cancer. Even condoms, often praised as a means of protection against certain sexually transmitted diseases, give little more than a false sense of security. In actual practice in the real world, they are only about 87% effective even in avoiding *pregnancy and STDs.*

The unrestricted sexual pleasure of marital sexual intercourse is a mutual *gift,* willed by God. Each spouse should actually try to make the experience as pleasurable as possible for the *other,* bringing the two of them closer as a result, and making them fully aware, through their senses, of the profound meaning of the act itself. Contraception, in contrast, infallibly leads each person to isolate, and focus on, what can be *taken* from the act, so that pleasure becomes no longer a means, but an obstacle, to true union. As each person has already decided to reject an integral dimension (i.e., the fertility) of the other, true, *ecstatic* union is no longer possible, and one's body, and even one*self,* meant to be a gift to be given, becomes an object to be used.

Sexual pleasure, a good to be generously enjoyed

Catholic tradition has long defended the need to preserve the true enjoyment and spontaneity of marital sexual intercourse. St Thomas Aquinas, in fact, was once challenged with the objection that sexual pleasure, or passion, was always sinful, because it was always immoderate. His students apparently wondered whether sexual pleasure might itself be sinful, a vice, because it had such a powerful effect on one's ability to think clearly. St Thomas responded that a passion only amounts to a vice, not just when it is *intense,* but only when it is no longer *subject to reason.*[14] He observed that no matter how intense the passionate pleasure of lawful sexual intercourse may be, it can still always be subject to reason, not

the Catholic view on sexual pleasure is that it ought to be ecstatic

in the sense that one can reason about it during the act itself, but that one can reason *beforehand* that it is good to engage in this act with this person at this time. In essence, sexual intercourse, according to St Thomas, is the one area in which the reasonable and virtuous thing to do is to consent to reason's being, as it were, "overwhelmed," for a moment, by passion. As St Thomas' reflection reveals, the Catholic view on sexual pleasure is that it ought to be *ecstatic.*

Sexual pleasure is *never* sinful in fact, except by association with a sexual *act* that is itself sinful. Pleasure isn't something we *do,* but something that *happens* in us; and only what we *do* - or fail to *do* - can ever be sinful. The experience of pleasure, however, must be properly integrated into the true context of the sexual act, and cannot become its ultimate *goal.* Pleasure is meant to

---

[14] Aquinas, *In IV Sententiae,* dist. 31, q. 2, a. 1, ad 3.

assist the goals of human sexuality, which are to unite the spouses and to participate with God in the creation of new persons. "Pleasure," *in itself,* is never one of the *purposes* of human sexuality, anymore than the icing is the purpose for the cake.

The truth is, pleasure cannot become the *goal* of sexual intercourse without creating a situation in which at least one of the persons will be end up being "used" by the other. The integration of sexual pleasure in authentic marital sexual intercourse is perfected when each spouse seeks to *give* as much pleasure as possible to the other as an expression of the gift of oneself. Put another way, sexual pleasure is something to be enjoyed *generously,* not *selfishly.* (Given certain physical differences between a man and woman, the giving of pleasure to each other with true charity requires a degree of continence, or self-control, *especially on the part of the man,* that is related to growth in the virtue of chastity; cf. *LR* 270 ff.)

5. THEOLOGICAL REQUIREMENTS

How a Marriage *Comes to Be* Permanent

Marriage is a covenant, a commitment in faith. It is also, therefore, sometimes called a contract, especially when, in canon and civil law, it is helpful to codify some of its terms. The term "marriage," in fact can refer to two distinct realities: the act of consent, including consummation, by which the marriage of a man and a woman *comes to be,* and the stable community of life and love built around the resulting bond between them, that is, marriage as a *lived reality.* The community (and the bond) that results from entering into marriage is not static; it is a dynamic presence of the Holy Spirit, a constant fountain of the grace of which the sacrament of matrimony is an effective sign.

Consent

The complex action by which a Catholic marriage comes to be has four elements: consent, consummation, public recognition, and the blessing of the Church. The difference between the consent that makes a marriage, and the promise that, in times past, made a betrothal, is the difference between present and future. (Sometimes such "betrothals," in times past, were judged to be valid, but only once the marriage was consummated.) The consent that makes a marriage is immediately effective. By it, a man and a woman mutually surrender themselves to each other for the rest of their lives.

Today, this consent is normally given in a formula of words. In the past, it was sometimes given simply by the presence of the couple in the ceremony and by their use of certain signs, such as an exchange of rings. It is not the expression of the consent that matters, as much as the consent itself, and the fact that everyone knows that this is what is taking place.

Consummation

From the moment of consent, the right to consummate the marriage begins immediately to exist. For very serious reasons, a couple may decide not to consummate a marriage, and still be a validly married couple. For example, Mary and Joseph were truly married; they never consummated their marriage, and Mary remained perpetually a virgin. Normally, however, spouses, by expressing their consent, are also expressing their intent to ratify their consent by consummating their marriage.

 The complex action by which a Catholic marriage comes to be has four elements:

- consent,
- consummation,
- public recognition,
- and the blessing of the Church.

Public Recognition

Public recognition of a marriage, through the person of the priest (or deacon) and the witnesses, goes together with the fact that the missions contained in the *original nuptial blessing* are missions that belong to the whole Church, and with the fact that marriage itself is a sacrament of communion, ordered to the salvation of others. (The Church does, for grave and urgent reasons, permit "secret" marriages, although the secret is never binding on the Ordinary (usually, the Bishop), who may divulge it at any time in order to avoid grave scandal or harm to the sanctity of marriage (cf. *CCL* 1130-33)).

Normally, this public recognition is fulfilled in the person of an official witness of the Church, and two other witnesses. The official witness is normally a priest, or a deacon, but in extreme circumstances, the local Bishop, with permission of the Holy See, may appoint a lay man or woman to assist at marriage ceremonies in the name of the Church (*CCL* 1112). In situations of even more extreme difficulty, however, when there is danger of death, or when it will not be possible for at least one month to find someone competent and authorised to assist at their marriage, a couple may be validly and licitly married by pronouncing their consent merely in the presence of two witnesses (cf. *CCL* 1116). (These extreme situations typically occur only in mission territories or in time of persecution.)

The Blessing of the Church

The nuptial blessing, given by the Church, is an invocation to God to send the Holy Spirit, who is Love Itself, upon the newly married spouses, to fill them and give life to their marriage (cf. *MD* 29; *LF* 4).

A Permanent Result

Once consent is given, the couple is married. The consummation of their marriage ratifies the consent already given; it reinforces the indissolubility of the marriage, completes its symbolism, and fulfils its supernatural meaning as a source of grace. Through the consummation, the man and woman, already married, become truly "one flesh" with each other, and "one Spirit" with the Holy Spirit and the Church. The Church has never held that a valid, consummated marriage between baptised persons can be dissolved for any reason, by any human power.

What Makes a Marriage a Sacrament

The Baptism of Both Spouses

The baptism of the two spouses is what makes Christian marriage a sacrament. Unlike other sacraments, it is not so easy - or useful - to employ technical terminology of "matter" (i.e., the essential gestures) and "form" (i.e., the essential words) to describe the elements of the sacrament of Matrimony; it is perhaps easier, and more instructive, to speak of Matrimony simply as a sacrament in which the effects of Baptism, especially its character, are extended in a special way to the entire life of the couple. The usual blessing of the marriage by a priest is not the "form" of the sacrament, for the spouses are both *ministers* and *subjects* of the sacrament, each one administering the sacrament to the other.

> *the spouses are both ministers and subjects of the sacrament, each one administering the sacrament to the other*

The grace of the sacrament is produced through the personal action of Christ. The man and woman, as ministers, represent Christ to each other within his Mystical Body. Christ will always perform the action of the sacrament when all conditions for it are met; he does not depend on the man and the woman, as ministers of it, to be holy. If they are holy, however, they can be for each other an additional channel of his grace. Future spouses owe it *to each other* to be very close to God on their wedding day; a good confession beforehand can reap benefits for a lifetime together.

A Precise Intention

As ministers, the spouses must have the precise *intention* "to do what the Church does" for the sacrament to be valid. Intention is not the same as attention. Most people get distracted on their wedding day, but that does not affect the validity of the sacrament. As ministers of the sacrament, however, they should also take care to celebrate the sacrament *licitly,* that is, in accord with the way that the Church asks it to be celebrated, even in its non-essential elements. Neither orthodox faith, however, nor good moral dispositions, are necessary for the sacrament to be *valid,* although they are necessary to receive it *worthily,* and for the *grace* of the sacrament to be received in its fulness.

Freedom from Impediments

For a marriage to be a valid covenant, or contract, both spouses must have the mental and physical *capacity* to enter into marriage, and they must be *free,* as well as having the *intention* to administer and receive the sacrament according to the intention of the Church (cf. *CCC* 1625 ff). They must not be under any fear or constraint; they must also have the capacity to enter into a marriage and to fulfill its obligations, free (or, at least, dispensed) from any impediments. These impediments, which are fully listed in the Canon Law of the Church (*CCL* 1083-1107) are based on requirements that the intended spouses be of a certain age; that they have the (physical) ability to engage successfully in sexual intercourse, and the (psychological) ability to do so *with each other;* that they be free from commitments such as prior marriages or religious consecration; that they not be too closely related, even if by adoption or illegitimacy; and other requirements of general good faith. Because the fruitfulness of a marriage can take many forms, however, sterility is *not* in itself an impediment.

Mixed Marriages

One other impediment worth consideration is that which arises when one of the intended spouses is Catholic, and the other is not, but has been baptised. This is the case of the "mixed marriage." Because of the great *mystery* that a marriage between baptised persons is, and the way that it is ordered to the life of the Church, the local Ordinary (usually the Bishop) *may* grant a dispensation to allow the marriage if there is a "just and reasonable cause," and if the following three conditions are met: the Catholic must make a declaration of intent to preserve his own faith, and promise to do everything possible to baptise the children and bring them up in the Catholic Church, the non-Catholic must be completely aware of these responsibilities of the Catholic, and both of them must be fully instructed regarding "the purposes and essential properties of marriage" (*CCL* 1125; cf. 1124-29). If all of the prescribed conditions are met, a sacramental marriage is the result. Nevertheless, "the difficulties of mixed marriages must not be underestimated" (*CCC* 1634; cf. 1633-37).

Disparity of Cult

A similar impediment arises when one of the intended spouses is Catholic, and the other has never been baptised at all. This is known as a situation of "disparity of cult." Unless a dispensation similar to that of a mixed marriage is given, with the same three conditions, any marriage will be invalid. Even if the dispensation is given, however, the result will still not be a sacramental marriage. The person who is not baptised can neither give, nor receive, the sacrament, and so neither one receives it.

Although this point is still debated theologically, the Church has routinely dissolved consummated marriages between a baptised person (especially a non-Catholic) and an unbaptised person, "in favour of the faith," for example, when one of the parties converts to the Catholic Church and the other actively opposes the conversion. The argument from the *practice* of the Church, then, which has essentially resolved the question, is: If these marriages were *sacraments,* they would be indissoluble. The Church dissolves them. Therefore, they are natural marriages, for they are dissoluble.

The difficulties in a situation of "disparity of cult" may be expected to be even greater than those of a mixed marriage. God will still assist the couple in the requirements of their state in life - in fact, the Catholic spouse will in some way unite the other to the Church (cf. *1 Cor* 7:14) - but they will not be full participants in the *mystery* of a sacramental marriage.

The Natural vs. the Supernatural Order

Every marriage, as a reflection of the original blessing, is *ordered,* in and of itself, to the grace of God. *Not every* marriage actually realises the full participation in the grace of God to which it is ordered. To those who are members of the Church, and participate in the sacraments, only sacramental marriage is possible; to those who are not baptised, only natural marriage is possible. Every natural marriage, however, is potentially a sacramental marriage[15]; if two unbaptised spouses receive the sacrament of Baptism, they will also begin to experience the grace of the *sacrament* of Matrimony, at once. Their marriage may be blessed, if they so wish, but it is already valid; it has become a sacrament, like every marriage, by virtue of their *baptism.*

On the other hand, two baptised persons who marry in a merely civil union are not considered validly married *at all* by the Church, not even only naturally. Marriage is an intimate community of life and love, based on a full and mutual self-surrender. Their baptism, however, has left in each of them a sacramental *character,* a permanent seal that marks them as belonging to the Body of Christ. It is impossible for two baptised persons to surrender themselves completely to each other, so as to form such an intimate community, if they each act as if their

---

[15] Cf. Aquinas, *In IV Sententiarum* dist. 39, q. 1, a. 2, ad 1.

baptism, an intimate dimension of themselves, was and is utterly meaningless. Yet that is what they do, if they attempt to marry without giving or receiving the *sacrament* of Matrimony, which extends the character of Baptism to the entire relationship. Leaving out such an essential dimension of themselves from their commitment to each other, even if it is because they themselves each reject this dimension, they do not fulfill the conditions even for a natural marriage to begin.

The Church does recognise, from a pastoral perspective, that their situation cannot be compared to that of two persons living together without any bond at all, for there is at least some sort of commitment to a concrete, maybe even stable, form of life together (although, by their action, they have left open the possibility of divorce). Nevertheless, it is simply not enough to succeed in forming an intimate community of life and love, even on the natural level (*FC* 82). No two baptised persons can ever validly contract marriage with each other except through the sacrament (*CCL* 1055).

Indissolubility

Once a marriage has been validly contracted, it is *internally* indissoluble (that is, the actual marriage *bond* is indissoluble), according to the order in which the marriage was contracted. A sacramental marriage is *supernaturally* indissoluble, that is, the two spouses have been joined together by God. Even a natural marriage, however, is *naturally* indissoluble, that is, it is *naturally* ordered to permanence; and indeed, there is a natural demand for permanence in every conjugal relationship:

> Sexuality, by means of which man and woman give themselves to one another through the acts which are proper and exclusive to spouses, is by no means something purely biological, but concerns the innermost being of the human person as such. It is realised in a truly human way only if it is an integral part of the love by which a man and a woman commit themselves totally to one another until death. The total physical self-giving would be a lie if it were not the sign and fruit of a total personal self-giving, in which the whole person, including the temporal dimension, is present: if the person were to withhold something or reserve the possibility of deciding otherwise in the future, by this very fact he or she would not be giving totally (*FC* 11).

Dissolutions

Every valid marriage is indissoluble. Yet, there are certain cases in which the Church does have the authority actually *to dissolve* a marriage. A sacramental marriage, *once consummated,* can only be dissolved by the death of the one of the spouses (cf. *CCL* 1141). *Before* it is consummated, however, at the request of one of the spouses, and for a just reason, it may be still be *dissolved* by the Pope, for the entire set of actions by which a marriage *comes to be* has not yet been *fully* carried out (cf. *CCL* 1142). In other cases, the Church may also *dissolve* a natural marriage in favour of a supernatural principle, that is, for the sake of the faith.

The Pauline Privilege

One of these principles is known as the *pauline privilege,* as it is based on a passage from the letters of St Paul:

> The rest is from me and not from the Lord. If a brother has a wife who is an unbeliever, and she is content to live with him, he must not send her away; and if a woman has an unbeliever for her husband, and he is content to live with her, she must not leave him. This is because the unbelieving husband is made one with the saints through his wife, and the unbelieving wife is made one with the saints through her husband. If this were not so, your children would be unclean, whereas in fact they are holy. However, if the unbelieving partner does not consent, they may separate; in these circumstances, the brother or sister is not tied: God has called you to a life of peace. If you are a wife, it may be your part to save your husband, for all you know; if a husband, for all you know, it may be your part to save your wife (*1 Cor* 7:12-16; cf. *CCL* 1143).

This privilege applies when only one of two unbaptised spouses receives baptism. The other spouse has not been baptised, and so their marriage has not become a sacrament. If the unbelieving spouse "departs" from the baptised spouse, the baptised spouse is free to marry, and at the moment that he contracts a sacramental marriage, the natural marriage is, by the fact of the new marriage, dissolved in its favour. The unbaptised spouse is considered to have "departed" if he is unwilling to live with the baptised spouse, or, unwilling "to live peacefully without offence to the Creator" (for example, by insisting on a continued use of contraception), unless the baptised spouse has himself given the other spouse a reason to "depart," for example, by committing adultery after his conversion. The Church is very careful, when applying this privilege, to preserve the rights of the unbaptised spouse; once applied, however, the baptised person is free to marry. Very rarely, and for grave reasons, the Church may apply this privilege in order to permit a mixed marriage or another marriage to an unbaptised person (one who presumably would be more favourable to the Catholic faith of the baptised) (cf. *CCL* 1143-47).

The Petrine Privilege

Indissolubility is one of the properties of a valid marriage. The other is unity. The second principle according to which the Church may dissolve a valid marriage in favour of the faith applies when the unity of marriage has not been respected. This principle, often called the *petrine privilege,* applies in the case of a polygamous, unbaptised spouse who converts to the faith. Normally, that spouse would remain married to the first of his spouses, and dismiss the others. If there would be a hardship for him to remain with the first, however, he may choose to retain *one* of the others instead, in favour of the faith. In either case, the local bishop must ensure that adequate provision is also made for the needs of the other spouses (cf. *CCL* 1148).

A second application of the *petrine privilege* occurs when a newly baptised person cannot be reunited with an unbaptised spouse because of captivity or persecution. The person may be permitted to enter into a sacramental marriage with someone else, even if the other person has received baptism in the meantime, while they were apart. The preference, in the application of the *petrine principle,* is always to act in favour of the faith (*CCL* 1149-50).

Divorce

Because marriage is indissoluble, the Catholic Church does not permit or recognise divorce, which is an attempt to break a marriage apart through merely legal force. The Church does recognise the occasional need for *separation,* that is, for spouses to live apart, no longer sharing bed and board, or cohabiting, especially when one of the spouses has been unfaithful to the marriage (cf. *Matt* 19:9), or is a physical or moral danger to the other. For grave reasons, the legal action known as "divorce" may sometimes be employed as a last resort by a Catholic spouse as a way to give a *separation* legal force. An example of a last resort might be to ensure certain legal rights, to provide for children, or to protect an inheritance (cf. *CCC* 2383; 2382-86).

Normally, the Church has opposed laws that permit "divorce," for they give false testimony regarding the natural indissolubility of a marriage. In cultures where "divorce" is common, however, some legal systems may be set up in such a way that recourse to "divorce" as a legal procedure may be the only prudent means of enforcing a just separation, for instance, to protect one of the spouses from serious abuse by the other, or to ensure legal provision for the needs of children. Such a protective use of "divorce" law, however, should be a last resort, and should be done very discreetly. Although "divorce" is really a legal fiction, the fiction itself increases the temptation of the spouses to consider their bond dissolved, which it is not, and to seek comfort outside of their marriage, which still exists. The apparent "divorce" is also a source of scandal to others, who will naturally consider it an attempt to dissolve the marriage. Finally, it impedes the eventual reconciliation of the spouses, by requiring them legally to "re-marry."

Sometimes the term "external indissolubility," is used in this context. This is a technical term that is easily misunderstood. Normally, a valid marriage is indissoluble both internally (with respect to the bond of communion), and externally (with respect to the spouses actually living together). External indissolubility is a mere reflection of internal indissolubility, and it may be suspended for a time for a grave reason, and for the good of the persons involved. One may occasionally encounter this term, but, because it can be quite confusing to speak of the "merely external dissolution" of a marriage, it is far better simply to use the term, "separation." The meaning is the same; the *marriage* still exists.

Even when a merely legal "divorce" is employed in this fashion, both spouses must remain faithful to each other, even while separated, remembering that, in spite of the legal fiction of "divorce," the marriage itself continues. The legally "divorced" spouses must not attempt to contract new marriages to someone else, for, in God's eyes, they are still married to each other until one of them dies. If one of them "remarries" while the other is alive, he places himself in a situation of objective contradiction toward his own body (he is one flesh with his "first" - and only - spouse), and toward the Holy Spirit that unites him through his "first" spouse to the Church. As long as his situation remains so, he may not receive Christ in the Eucharist, which, as an effective sign of communion with the Body of Christ, is intimately related, for him, to the bond that unites him to his actual spouse.

Annulments

Any marriage is absolutely indissoluble by any human authority, whether civil or ecclesiastical, whenever three conditions have been met: the two spouses were baptised before marriage; they entered freely and validly into marriage, intending that their marriage be permanent, and that it be open to procreation; and they engaged in at least one act of natural, that is, *non-contraceptive,* intercourse after marriage.

In certain cases, the Church may grant an *annulment* of a marriage that everyone presumed before to be valid, perhaps even for many years. There can be many reasons for granting an annulment, which is a statement by the Church that the couple did not manage successfully to complete the set of actions by which the marriage would have *come to be.* Some annulments are granted because, due to an impediment, full, true consent was never actually given. Other annulments are granted because a marriage was never successfully consummated.

Surprisingly to some, many marriages may not have been consummated, even after several years, because contraception was always used during intercourse. Contraceptive intercourse, which divides the spouses instead of uniting them, is not a conjugal act, and *does not consummate a marriage.* Marriage is consummated *only* by a truly human, conjugal act, that is, an act open to life and love, and not by a merely genital act between persons who happen to be married (*CCL* 1061, §1).

Annulments are not a form of "Catholic divorce." They are, instead, a declaration by the Church that the marriage never existed; what appeared to be a marriage, did not quite satisfy the requirements to become one. That does not mean, however, that the two persons were living in sin, if they were acting in good faith all along, thinking that they were married. Annulments, when finally granted, should be accepted in faith, and not resisted; the intention behind granting them is to help persons to live in the truth.

The Church's granting of annulments actually reinforces its teaching on the sanctity and indissolubility of marriage by emphasising the specific conditions that are necessary for a marriage actually to begin. Marriage is more than a ceremony, and a wedding is more than a reception and a honeymoon. Careful, prayerful, honest and chaste preparation for the reception of the sacrament of Matrimony helps not only to receive it worthily and well, but also to minimise the need for future annulments.

CHRISTIAN MARRIAGE: A TIMELESS MYSTERY

Marriage between a man and a woman reflects an eternal mystery that is fully realised in Christian marriage. The mystery is timeless, and much too profound to be changed or affected by mere cultural circumstances. We, however, are conditioned by the times in which we live, and so it is helpful to encounter an expression of this mystery that is more understandable for us today.

The Mystery in the Witness of Married Couples

The most compelling proof of God's loving presence in our lives is to "meet" Him in those who, through their fidelity to His plan, have grown most like him, and most reflect his love. Most of us, if we reflect about it, have probably known persons, and especially married couples, who have witnessed to us in this way.

The Church has long had the practice of holding the lives of holy persons up for others to emulate. These are the saints, who inspire us with their fidelity to the plan of God over their lives. Recently, the Church has begun to seek to recognise the sanctity of married couples *together,* recognising that the marriage community of life and love in which they lived was their way to holiness.

Two of these couples are Luigi Quattrocchi and Maria Corsini, a couple who "lived an extraordinary life in an extraordinary way,"[16] and Louis Stanislaus Martin and Marie Zelie Guérin, parents of St Thérèse of Lisieux, the "little flower," who learned a profound and simple way of loving God, largely through emulating the love of her parents. Pope John Paul has recently honoured both couples by advancing them closer to being canonised as saints.

Sacred Scripture also gives us many examples of couples to emulate for their trustful surrender to the love of God. Among these are Abraham and Sarah, Tobias and Sarah, Zechariah and Elisabeth, and Joseph and Mary. The marriage of Joseph and Mary, which was a real marriage although never consummated, was made fruitful in its *legal* offspring, Jesus, who, as the Son of God, and the Son of Mary, was also the adopted son of Joseph. Yet, through faith, both Mary and Joseph were also the adopted children of God. The Holy Family of Jesus, Mary, and Joseph is a model for all marriages and families to become communities of life and love built around the Life and Love of God.

The Mystery in Our Own Lives

By reflecting on these excellent examples, we may find ourselves inspired to draw even closer to God, as they

---

[16] Pope John Paul II, *Homily on the Occasion of the Beatification of the Servants of God Luigi Beltrame Quattrocchi and Maria Corsini, Married Couple* (Sunday, 21 October 2001).

did. God never changes, and the examples of those who have become, in some way, a reflection of God, are valid for all time. Through prayer, we can also speak to them, and develop a close and intimate friendship with them, that will assist us to live our own vocations in life. They will infallibly lead us to grow closer to our truest Friend, who is Jesus, the Bridegroom, who pursues each of us with an eternal Love that is the Source and Inspiration for all true romantic love.

FURTHER READING

Works by Pope John Paul II

Apostolic Exhortation *Redemptoris Custos* (15 August 1989).
Apostolic Exhortation *Christifidelis Laici* (30 December 1988).
Apostolic Letter *Mulieris Dignitatem* (15 August 1988).
Apostolic Exhortation *Familiaris Consortio* (22 November 1981).
Encyclical Letter *Evangelium Vitae* (15 March 1995).
Letter to Families (2 February 1994).
Letter to Women (29 June 1995).
The Theology of the Body: Human Love in the Divine Plan.
    Boston: Pauline Books and Media, 1997.

Works by Karol Wojtyla *(before becoming Pope)*

Fruitful and Responsible Love. New York: The Seabury Press
    (Crossroad), 1979.
Love and Responsibility. Translated by T. H. Willets. San
    Francisco: Ignatius Press, 1993 (originally published in 1960).
"The Jeweller's Shop," in *The Collected Plays and Writings on
    Theater,* tr. B. Taborski (Berkeley: University of California
    Press, 1987), pp. 267-322.
"The Problem of Catholic Sexual Ethics: Reflections and Postulates"
    (pp. 279-99), "The Teaching of the Encyclical *Humanae Vitae*
    on Love: An Analysis of the Text" (pp. 301-14), "The Family as
    a Community of Persons" (315-27), "Parenthood as a
    Community of Persons," (pp. 329-42), and "Pastoral Reflections
    on the Family" (pp. 343-61), in *Person and Community: Selected*

Essays. Translated by Theresa H. Sandok, O.S.M. Catholic Thought From Lublin, 4. New York: Peter Lang, 1993.

"The Truth of the Encyclical Humanae Vitae." *L'Osservatore Romano,* Weekly Edition in English, 16 January 1969, p. 6.

Magisterial Works

Catechism of the Catholic Church, nos. 1601-1666.

Code of Canon Law (1983), nos. 1055-1165.

Sacred Congregation for the Doctrine of the Faith, *Persona Humana: Declaration on Certain Questions Concerning Sexual Ethics* (29 December 1975).

Second Vatican Ecumenical Council, Pastoral Constitution on the Church in the Modern World *Gaudium Et Spes* (7 December 1965), nos. 47-52.

Other Works

Hogan, Richard M., and John M. LeVoir. *Covenant of Love: Pope John Paul II on Sexuality, Marriage, and Family in the Modern World.* San Francisco: Ignatius Press, 1992.

Olsen, Glenn W. (ed.), *Christian Marriage: A Historical Study.* New York: Crossroad, 2001.

Pope Paul VI, Encyclical Letter *Humanae Vitae* (25 July 1968)

Shivanandan, Mary. *Crossing the Threshold of Love. A New Vision of Marriage in the Light of John Paul II's Anthropology.* Washington, D.C.: The Catholic University of America Press, 1999.

On the Sacraments

Baptism (CTS Publications, 2004; Do 712).

Confirmation (CTS Publications, 2004; Do 713).

Eucharist (CTS Publications, 2004; Do 714).
Reconciliation (CTS Publications, 2004; Do 716).
Anointing (CTS Publications, 2004; Do 711).
Marriage (CTS Publications, 2004; Do 710).
Holy Orders (CTS Publications, 2004; Do 715).

Abbreviations used in this book

CCC *Catechism of the Catholic Church.*

CCL *Code of Canon Law,* 1983.

FC Pope John Paul II, Apostolic Exhortation *Familiaris Consortio* (22 November 1981).

GS Second Vatican Ecumenical Council, Pastoral Constitution on the Church in the Modern World *Gaudium Et Spes* (7 December 1965).

LF Pope John Paul II, *Letter to Families* (2 February 1994).

LR Karol Wojtyla, *Love and Responsibility,* tr. H. Willetts (San Francisco: Ignatius, 1993).

MD Apostolic Letter *Mulieris Dignitatem* (15 August 1988).

TB Pope John Paul II, *The Theology of the Body: Human Love in the Divine Plan* (Boston: Pauline Books and Media, 1997).

Informative Catholic Reading

We hope that you have enjoyed reading this booklet.

If you would like to find out more about CTS booklets - we'll send you our free information pack and catalogue.

Please send us your details:

Name ....

Address ....

....

....

Postcode ....

Telephone...

Email ....

Send to: CTS, 40-46 Harleyford Road,
          Vauxhall, London
          SE11 5AY

Tel: 020 7640 0042
Fax: 020 7640 0046
Email: info@cts-online.org.uk